Free Web Hosting

Hosting

Secrets

Terms and Conditions

Table Of Contents

Foreword

Cost is a predominant factor is almost all endeavors today and web hosting is not exactly exempted for this either. Therefore in the interest of trying to save on cost the option of using free web hosting becomes more attractive and usable. Get all the info you need here.

Secrets To Free Web Hosting

Everything You Need To Know About Choosing A Free Web Host

Chapter 1:

Web Host Basics

Synopsis

Besides the obvious factor of no cost, another advantage of free web hosting is that most will provide the customer base with pre made website layouts. These layouts are all design for immediate and ready to use purposes which electively eliminates the need to having to design one personally. This is quite beneficial for those with limited knowledge in this particular area.

The Basics

Basic knowledge of design, software and other beneficial know how elements would actually be needed in order to be able to set up an effective website. Thus the added advantage of having a predesigned site available for immediate use, becomes even more attractive a feature to consider.

However along with the advantages there are also very visible disadvantages especially when something is free. One of these disadvantages would come in the form of having to be part of already overcrowded servers.

This is an evident situation brought on by the fact that the web hosting is free, thus attracting those who are cost conscious and less knowledgeable in this area. This overcrowded situation often causes some down time on the web pages which is an unattractive result.

Most times the features offered are far less by comparison to paying web site hosts. Features such as emails, advance software options are often not included in free webhost facilities and designs. However for a newbie these are not very significant negative features.

The free webhosting platform does not normally offer customer service of any kind and this could be a very big disadvantage for those just starting out in the online foray. Without the avenue available to address problems or even be notified of such problems, this particular point could be very damaging to a newbie.

Chapter 2:

Synopsis

Although most would not advocate using the free web space there are some advantages that are worth exploring in this area. The main reason for not taking this particular tool seriously is the fact that it does not allow profit making business opportunities to be listed. It mainly caters to postings that involve nonprofit platforms. However the web space can still be used for attracting traffic to the primary site.

Size

The free webspace usually comes with tools that are needed to facilitate the quick and easy wetting up of a page. The tools given also help to make the eventual end design look more professional and attention grabbing.

These may include design options, layout options, page counters, guest books and a few other complimenting features. Although the space offered is quite limited, it adequately caters to the creation of a simple page that can showcase one or more products or elements about the business endeavor or simply offer a set of listing for further information.

This will effectively allow the individual to gain more traffic to the site thus helping indirectly to encourage the same said traffic to venture further to the actual main site. Being included in the host's directory of sites will also help to further the prospect of garnering more traffic as the host will usually ensure the traffic is drive to the featured sites.

The following are steps to use to find free web space:

- Use the search engine to find a reputable web host that offers free webspace.

- Researching what is available and choosing the one that most suits the needs of the individual should be next. This space usually is within the range of 10 megabytes to 5 gigabytes.

- Signup with the chosen webhost using an active email address, and the username and password will be sent through the inbox after the initial signup exercise is finished.

- Log in and start featuring the intended material designed for the site.

Chapter 3:

Synopsis

There is really very little that can actually be termed "free" in the online marketing platform and although there is such a thing as free web hosting there are also other connotations linked to the "free" tag. Therefore it should be understood that the free host tag does come with a price though not necessarily in terms of dollars.

What About Ads

The free web hosting site still has to pay for their service set up and continued functioning of the site, therefore the revenue to do so, has to come from somewhere. This usually comes in the form of advertisers who are interested in posting their ads at the said free site.

This also means that the said ads are going to be featured on the individual's site, without any need for consultation or approval from the said individual.

The individual will have no control over the postings at the site and this may or may not work as an advantage to the individual's own content postings.

For some the time and effort taken to design their own content is not worth the intrusion of other ads and content, especially if it is going to eventually overshadow the individual's posting.

This is basically one way of really understanding that there is nothing that is really free. Because of the no cost involved in being a part of the free web host, the individual will have no choice but to accept and hope that the other elements posted at the space will be less overwhelming and more beneficial to the individual's own agenda.

For some this scenario is acceptable because they are only interested in using the free host site as an experimental phase or a testing ground, for their endeavors, thus the other elements are not really something they would be overly concerned about.

Chapter 4:

Research FTP Access

Synopsis

FTP is also referred to as file transfer protocol or the transfer of tiles into a place where is can be accessed, downloaded and uploaded. This is a secure and simple way to send and receive files. If the individual intends to download a file from the internet and create a website with it then the FTP is exactly the tool for the exercise.

FTP

Initially the files are downloaded to an FTP server which should have a fairly large memory capacity to host the intended files the FTP server should have this so that the transfer can take place without any hitch.

The files can be accessed through any internet browser or any FTP software. Most of these files are available for only a short period of time and only a select few are available on a permanent base.

Accessing the files directly through the FTP address which is listed as ftp:// can be done by logging in with an ID and password.

The FTP site is usually file structured and similar to the "My Documents" on any computer and this is usually set up by an administrator.

These files may be public or private in nature and the access may include adding, moving, editing and deleting so if any of these functions do not respond to the related commands then the administrator should be informed.

Considering the FTP client is something that would create easy and regular access that is comparatively hassle free for uploads and downloads.

This would require the simple steps of drag and drop. All the frequented FTP sites and their corresponding logins and passwords can be stored conveniently in one place. Checking out the various resources available would allow the individual to make an informed decision on which one to choose that would best suit the needs.

- 15 -

Chapter 5:

Synopsis

An adequate list of free file hosting services can usually be found quite easily on the directory provided for such searches. Basically is provides for file storage and services by using bidirectional communications such as the internet network to transmit data to the server periodically or when needed.

Types Etc.

The user has very little limitations and can upload different sizes and types of documents such as photos, documents, files and information.

Here the tools are provided for such facilitation of downloading and uploading files to the shared with other respectively. There is usually no policy in place to charge the user and typically the service provider would be the one to welcoming the users to register and commence their posting immediately. As each provider has different conditions and terms of use the onus in on the individual to check the requirements well before signing up.

Most of these limitations are in place to keep those interested in posting at the sites to design posts that are concise and to the point. Using a limited amount of space will enable many others to have and enjoy the opportunities to use the same free web host too.

It also ensures that some control is in place to govern the users commitment to the postings as those who are not really committed may end up abusing the so called free facility given.

Some of these limitations include tinier bandwidth over a fixed period and it does not allow hot linking to files.

Also there may not be facilities to certain link files such as MP3, MPEG and ZIP files, and there is no real guarantee that there will be accessible adequate uptime.

For some these limitations may not eventually be feasible for them to consider posting at the free web host and may consider other options.

Chapter 6:

Research Reliability And Speed Of Access

Synopsis

There are many free hosting web sites that tout themselves as being free but in reality this is rarely the true picture. Some have hidden requirements while others facilitate tools that would require some kind of cost incurred when forced to use them. Therefore in short when it comes to the reliability issue linked to the free web host, this feature has rather negative connotations linked to it.

Is It Good

Generally viewed as not being reliable there are however a few exceptions to the rule, though really few and far between. If the host has avenue of creating revenue without actually having to impose on the individual seeking to post on the site, then in all likelihood there is little need to worry about it staying power.

However this is open to abuse and threat when those posting at the site indulge in spamming, hacking and other negative exercises which would eventually contribute to the overall problems at the site. These problems would include the server to experience a lot of down time or making the overall functions of the server comparatively slower.

This mostly happens when the webhost accept anyone and everyone with the automated instant activation system and offers features such as PHP or CGI. However all is not lost as the problems of reliability and speed access can be overcome with carefully selecting a free host that is conscientious about accepting only quality sites to host.

Different webhost have their own reliability and speed access issues but generally it all depends on the types of posting contents that will eventually dictate the two elements. However with certain criteria in place there is some control that can be exercised on the part of the webhost to ensure a reasonable level of reliability and speed access is evident.

Chapter 7:

Synopsis

PHP is basically a simpler version of Perl which is to say the latter is tailor made for the web with a more serious and involved programming language. However having both available for use can have its advantages, thus neither should be shunned over the other.

More Advanced

Most web application the use of PHP is really something that cannot be and should not be overlooked, as it is easy to learn and most forums, CMS, blogs and other interactive platforms make use of this form.

Almost everything else featured on the internet in some way of the other uses PHP too. Although it seems to be a given fact that PHP is now actively replacing Perl for web applications it will however most definitely not replace Perl for everything.

Most web programs can be easily written using PHP but writing a web server in one is almost impossible. Therefore the web server requires the use of Perl on all counts to create an effective and usable platform.

The following are some comparative points on the merits of Perl and PHP:

- Perl application using mod_perl are generally as fast is not faster that PHP application for most postings.

- PHP was originally written in Perl in the form of a module before the changes were made towards improvements.

- Perl has a very stable and mature database complete package which is DBI and it provides the database independent interface.

- PHP is missing many features that can be considered rather important to the serious language.

- PHP has a deliberate lack of advanced features and the web features that are currently included in the core language does make it easier to learn and use. Those without any programming experience can also easily use the PHP.

- Superficially both languages seem rather identical and Perl is not harder to read or use than PHP.

Chapter 8:

Synopsis

The bandwidth allotment would simply means an integrated product which provides a dynamic service when phone lines are not in use. This is done with the 1.5 Mbps of bandwidth becomes usable for the internet where traffic flow can be facilitated adequately.

Bandwidth

In its form it is a rather simplified networking tool that generally reduces costs and increases the efficiency rate. This is done when the IT burden is minimized through the reduction of IT support expenses. Form an installation point of view there is also the advantage of being somewhat flawless in nature.

There are generally no expected disruptions for the day to day running of the business engine. There is an integrated access device that is provided to ensure this consistent and prevailing situation. This is also usually provided at no additional cost to the individual.

For most keeping their existing phone numbers is a necessary and welcomed element and this in turn contributed to the further minimization of the overall expenses, as there is no hassle or disruption in the business which would usually occur when the numbers have to be changed.

As the numbers can be maintained it conveniently also means that all business cards, stationary , phone book listings and any other tools that would require the numbers to be featured would be able to remain without change thus saving on cost and time.

The proactive management of the network and troubleshooting elements are also another feature that the bandwidths can sufficiently handle at all times. This would allow the customer to feel at ease and have peace of mind.

All these are usually monitored and rectified before the impact is felt by the customer. With a full T1 platform there is no manipulation on the part of the bandwidth which would mean that there is fast internet usage that can be accessed anytime.

Chapter 9:

Extras Like Control Panel, Email, Forms, Etc

Synopsis

Diversification and offering complementing services and tools is always a welcomed element in any business garnering endeavor.

Adding on the mailbox feature to the web hosting package is relatively easy to do. These mail boxes are usually an addition to the already existing number of mail boxes that the individual already has with the initial package.

Needing additional server space to add to the functionality and upgrading standards of the features being offered at the website would also lend towards making the site more compatible, thus being able to sufficiently provide for this is an advantage.

Extras

Other extras that should be considered to be included would be the anti-virus and anti spam tools. These can provide invaluable service of protection for the site from website files that are constantly under threat of attack.

Using a dedicated IP address is also another feature encouraged as this would effective control the threat of having to deal with website problems that would occur if the website has been compromised through the blacklisted process.

The blacklisting can occur when the shared IP address has been misused by others using the same free webhost thus endangering the individual's own site.

Newer and dedicated web hosting plans and designs can be offered to loyal users as VPS or dedicated web hosting services. The cost involved may differ depending on the extent of the redesigning and sharing combinations.

This can be done without disturbing or compromising on the web quality as the new additions are incorporated in the system for the individual's use.

Wrapping Up

In order to stay competitive there is a constant need to explore feature that may provide added services to a customer base without any further cost or hassle to them. This is usually well received by the customer and keeps the webhost competitive and viable as a platform for providing free hosting features.

Do your homework and get started today.